Bite

The Pillow

poetry

by

Cheril N. Clarke

To everyone who supports me by liking, commenting, patronizing, and sharing my work online. Thank you. I appreciate you.

Table of Contents

Bite the Pillow is a multi-media poetry project. Scan the QR code below to watch visual versions of selected poems on my YouTube channel.

CHERIL N. CLARKE

Baptized in Pleasure

She leaves me breathless
Her touch
Her gaze
Her attention
They leave me in a state of liquidity
And vulnerability
I am shaken from my reality
My old self is transported through Calvary
She lifts me into a new realm – where I experience a rebirth
And I see Earth through a new lens
When I travel back, I know
That pleasure is everywhere.

Well Trained

It's different with him
I dominate
I control
I demonstrate
A power only endowed to those with fearless femininity
I use my stockings to make a leash and lead him on all fours
He follows my scent
Strides in my trail
He will follow me anywhere
His will has vanished into my exalted essence
Concatenated
He is my pet
Holding his breath until I tell him it's okay to breathe.

Duality

I am a masterpiece
I am glory
I am persistent pleasure
I am your conundrum if you are not ready
A magnificent problem if you are unsteady
I am a tundra ready for seed
A strait primed for the blending of open seas
Like honey being slowly poured down a spine
I am divine nectar
Uniquely designed
A delicacy your mind struggles to comprehend
Your God's send
I am your darkest desires and wildest fantasies
Can you handle my duality?

Make the Universe Tremble

My bedroom walls are black velvet
Aromatherapy pulses through the room like adrenaline
Tonight, I can be your medicine
But only if you let me.
I've outstretched my hand
To invite you in
Please
Come travel with me
Come go for a swim
Bringing fantasies to life is my specialty
I've created an atmosphere
Where time stops
I've erased the line of the horizon
Made gravity irrelevant
So we can keep rising
Made euphoria imminent
So we can go for hours
Past one
Past two
Past three
And even four orgasms...
Let's experience shockwaves of pleasure
And tremors of bliss
I've knocked the doors to other worlds off their hinges
With my intentions to sweep you into ecstasy
Grab ahold of me at the hips
Plunge into my rhythm
Feel our temperatures climb to a sizzle

As sweat drips down our necks
Grab my hair and tilt my head back
Watch me breathe as I ride
Watch me gasp as I writhe
Then let go
Allow me to regain control
Allow me to reign
Passive-aggressive
Enjoy this beautiful exchange
Indulge in my range, imbibe of my rain
Tonight, I want to make love so deeply
That we make the universe tremble.

Revival

She's so hungry for me
I feel my skin sizzle and tingle at the anticipation
Of her kiss.
Her bites.
Her licks.
I want to freeze the moment and live in it
Hold it for a century
Guard it like a sentry
I've searched and hunted for hundreds of years for this
Until I'd given up
Until I'd abandoned the desire to be desired
To be taken
I'd been so exhausted and bruised by the journey
That I simply didn't have the energy to proceed
But just when I thought I was on my last breath
I ambled into a rainforest under her reign
A femme-dom I could depend on for a revival
For a renewal.
For a reversal.
For rejuvenation.
Everything was love under her canopy of trees
Oxygen flowed freely
Desire for me was teeming
Life swung from serene to extreme and back again
And it was so
Damned
Freeing.

Suspended in Apprehension

I want to fall into your arms
And just be nurtured
But I can't let go
I am afraid.
I don't want to be too much
I don't want to say the wrong thing
I don't want to reveal too much of the real me
I don't want to overwhelm you with my passions and
emotions
And feelings
They run deep
They cast wide
I've been told I am a lot
I don't want to exhaust you
So, I've trained myself to restrain myself
But something about you is silently screaming at me to let go
and just be
But it's not that easy
I've slinked down to a speck of my potential
Placed myself behind a shield
I don't want to be too much
I don't want to be wounded
And I don't want to lose you.

She is Home

Her love is brilliant and dramatic
Thoughtful and constantly climatic
She is a field of ecstatic dreams
I run through her at sunrise
With glee
With thankfulness
With humility
She still gives me butterflies
She galvanizes my soul
Makes me whole
She is home.

CHERIL N. CLARKE

Submerged in a Debaucherous Queendom

The struggle is real
She's pulling me under
Deeply into wonder
Into her tender monarchy
Where the water is darker and colder
Where trust is paramount to survival
And I've sunken past familiar territory
Excitement and fear wash over me
I can't breathe
I've lost my composure
We're outside of my reality
In an aquatic enclosure
Of her construction and it's flooded
I've lost control
She is fascinated and invigorated by me in this state
I am entangled, impregnated and straight up inebriated
In the middle of the day
I don't know if this woman is poison or panacea.

She is Light

Nothing I've ever learned
Could have prepared me for her arrival
Into my world
Flippant and audacious
Unusual and bold
Unlike anyone I've ever met
She is a storm and doesn't even know it
Her presence has thrust me into a whirlwind of self-
examination
She has electrified my soul
Revived old dreams
Triggered streams of tears
Illuminated my fears
Peeled back layers
That had been buried for years
No longer can I roll, coast, and tumble in a void
She is a torchlight in the dark
Refusing to let me ignore the desperate moans of my soul.

CHERIL N. CLARKE

Desire

I want to get lost inside of you
The whirlwinds
The gentle breezes
The dawns and the dusks
The misfortunes and the luck
I want to untangle your contradictions
Unwrap your enigma
Pleasure map you until every inch is familiar
Relieve your pressures
Unearth your treasures
I want to make love to the entire essence of your being
Until you're free and believing
Reeling and teeming from my insatiable hunger for you.

Guiding Refuge

You are my sanctuary
I blossom in the crux of your embrace
Flourish at the thought of you
Even if we are oceans away
Or years apart
I've absorbed so much of your tenderness
That my heart will never feel your absence
You've soaked into the fabric of my soul
And unleashed me
You are my shepherd to freedom
I've seen the light of your queendom
A blue beacon in a red sky
I will follow the path to wherever it is leading
The jewel in your crown is my north star
You are my guiding refuge.

CHERIL N. CLARKE

On the Edge

Loving you
Is like standing on the edge of a cliff
Above choppy waters
There's danger
There's risk
It's like standing on the brink
Of freefalling into myself
Because of your constant encouragement
To live in fullness
To live fearlessly
In the beauty
In the mess
My toes are at the edge
Do I let go and let be
And let the waters below carry me
To freedom unleashed
To liberation?
Or do I pull away and run to safety
To what's familiar
No surprises no thriller
Just nagging whispers
I should've taken the risk.

Gates of Pleasure

This woman sweats rosewater
Her conversation
Her voice.
Her vibe.
She is intoxicating
She gives me chills
This woman is a rare find.
A goddess amongst stone statues
A force against immovable objects
She beckons.
She cracks open.
She is bewitching
This woman is heavenly
Her breath is a gentle heat against my skin
A vice to gently melt the ice
And pry me open
Her eyes bore into my soul
She sees me as I am
And who I can be
If I let my guard down
And open up the gates to pleasure.

Self-Love

The look and feel of self-love
Is evolving for me
The vision and scent of self-care
Is expanding for me
Farther along the quiet journey now
I can taste the ambrosia of freedom
It has satiated my soul
I've kissed the Spirit
Shared breath with the vivid
Divine reflection of my being
I've discovered my inner Garden of Eden
Through having the courage
To embrace myself wholly
Now can finally say, I love ALL of me.

She is Divine

Her eyes are diamonds
Stretched across the horizon
She is tethered to the heavens
Anchored by the ocean
She is infinity
The dark and light of the universe
Unafraid of herself
She embraces herself
She is a formidable strength
An uncommon confidence
She is defiant and
Too much for most
But just enough for me
Look into her soul and you'll see
The moon, the earth, and the sea
She is the mother, sister, daughter, lover, best friend all at
once
A foot soldier for love
My twin soul
She is the divine feminine.

CHERIL N. CLARKE

The Womb of Love

Her embrace is a respite for the weary
Shelter for the tired soul
So exhausted from running from life itself
I collapse into her lap
Onto the womb of love
I am relieved to find heaven on earth
In her.
In me.
In we.
When we are in sync…
Her gaze penetrates and uplifts
She heals with a glance
A touch
A kiss
A slow dance
She anchors me like gravity
I am so unsteady without her
She is light.
She is love.
She is home.
She is everything.

Mirror Work

I don't think she's an angel
Don't think she came from the sky or heaven
This woman is a root
A pillar
She is core
Boiling with passion and purpose
And heat
She is 37 trillion cells of intensity
The feeling of solidity in an uncertain world
She is a vibrating blend of ecstasy and complexity
Knowing it's okay to waver
To ebb
To flow
She is unapologetic
She gives zero fucks
She is aesthetic
From her depths stretching beyond her aura
Her field is MAGNETIC.
She is me when I am living comfortably in my skin.

CHERIL N. CLARKE

Feel and Just Be

This woman has shaken my world
She has fed my soul
She is a well of humanity
A swell of a spectrum
Quite the spectacle
In a world where everyone aims
To strip the fragility of our spirits
And pretend never to hurt
To never need to cry
To always be strong
To never crave the embrace of a friendly stranger
In their darkest hours
Because the pressures of life are too much
And they're suffocating amidst an abundance
While feeling lonely in a crowd
She floats in on a cloud
Reminding you that your soul is anchored to holy ground
She is a crown jewel
Inviting you to feel and just be.

Painkiller

I have to be careful with you
I'm liable to OD
You're stronger than X
Making my heart beat out of my chest
My breath… it hastens
My body yields and clings
Letting go and then folding inward
Confused
Overheated
Trembling
Shaking
Freezing
I want to make love to you inside the curve of a crescent
moon
With the light of the night at my back
And you daring me in delicious darkness at the front
Your ability to provide
A surgery of the spirit
Without an incision
To bring buried dreams to the surface like a vision
Makes you a hypnotic narcotic
Bringing me under
Where it's too deep to think clearly
Too deep to see what's ahead
Like too easily accessible fentanyl
You're a painkiller that can also kill.

Distant Lovers

I wish I could touch you tonight
Even a graze of my fingertips to your cheeks
Would do
As I lie in bed alone again
I find myself encapsulated by loving memories
Lost in vivid reveries
Of rocking and swaying with you
I wish I could feel you tonight
A forehead kiss
Or even a tender brush from your lips
Would do
I am craving your bliss.

I Refuse

I don't want to be the lonely woman in a crowded room
Beautifully disengaged
Distracted by the unexpected abandonment
Of love
And attention.
I don't want to be the girl with a shattered soul
Whose pieces all fell within
And cut into an already bleeding heart
That no one else can see
So they admire her from afar
Unable to hear her screams for more than a gaze
Her craving for even a simple touch
Even a graze of endearment.
I don't want to be the woman whose lips grip cigarettes
Suffocating her soul
Strangling her heart through labored and toxic breath
I refuse
I will not
I am too much of catch for that.

Surrender

Cover me in pleasure
The quiet kind that's slow and evenly paced
And full of breath...
Of both the subtle and strong breezes of life.
Envelope me in a honey-sweet euphoria
The kind that ebbs and flows
Stops and goes
That drips with the heat and slow intensity
Of candle wax.
Punctuate me passion
I want to feel your hunger for me and be ravished
Implant in me long-lasting orgasms that flutter for weeks
The kind that electrifies beyond the skin
To the depths of my spirit and lives within me.
Blanket me in unrestrained eroticism
The kind that's trained through discipline
To melt and congeal with me
To go slowly, heal and embed a sense of relief in me
I want to feel the tingle of your magnetic fields
Drawn into mine
As we hold each other and become one
I'm ready now
Ready to completely surrender to you.

Choose Love

People often ask me what's the secret
What are the things to say, do, or be
To love another person for 5,883 days (and counting)
The way that I've loved you
And you've loved me
With our entire souls
Our whole spirits
Our full beings
I could say, "open and honest communication"
But they often feel let down
As if it that's too cliché
Too trite
That it has to be more
I could say that I decided long ago
To be the wife and the mistress in my marriage
To embody the exotic
And perfect a pattern of conjuring fascination, foreignness
and intrigue
But the latter isn't what makes us work for the long-haul
Yes, it's beautiful, but it's also surface
There is no secret
Love isn't easy, but it is simple
It's daily commitment and action
So, I guess that's the answer... "the secret"
To Just
Choose
Love
Every

Day.
Be it. Commit to it.
To do whatever it takes to live up to the promises you made
to each other.
And most importantly, define it for yourselves
Individually and together
Grow and evolve through constant study and expanded
versions of self
Know that your union doesn't need to mirror any other
But it does need integrity, nurturing, inspection and
refinement
As the hurricanes of life will always be threats in the distance.

The Healer

She came into my life and rebuilt from the ruins
Left behind by the ungrateful
The unappreciative
The unaware
And the aloof
Brick by crumpled brick
She put me back together again
With love...and patience
Her embrace became my eternal refuge
Her gaze, a deluge
Of compassion
Cleansing my spirit of its languid mood
Strengthening my soul into a quiet sanctitude
Her impact is permanent.
She may be a dream
At least that's how it seems
But I'll never know
Because I won't dare try to see behind her seams.
Let her be a mirage.

Lonely Nights

I hold her pillow all night when she is gone
Clinging to the scent and imprint of her
Waiting for her to return from the firmament of solitude
I sleep restlessly
Tossing and turning like a restless sea
I dream recklessly
With weak and haggard breath
I miss my air
I wish she were here
I count the moments
Anxiously until she's back next to me.

Raw

Her eyes and smile bathe me like light
From a buttermilk sky
Rays of warmth raise my energy
Slow my heartbeat
And charge me centrally
Our lovemaking is art
A motion picture and still photography
It's hues and saturation
Truth and imagination
We snap together and shutter
Wrap around and melt into each other
We shudder and tremble
Crack open and reassemble anew
She captures me in action
In states of under and overexposure
{Vulnerable}
It's indecent how easily she sees me
Both conscious and unconscious
She teases me then leaves me
Alone
To develop in a dark room
With a sparked womb
Edging the background to the forefront
Uncropped, unfiltered, unmasked
Just raw.

CHERIL N. CLARKE

The Shaman

Sometimes life shrouds you in black smoke
And you feel trapped
You can't breathe
You can't see
And you don't want to feel
Because it hurts too much
I've been there
Almost lost myself, but she
She was my safety net
When I was free-falling in the dark
She was the light I fell into
She was the spark
The light that covered and protected me
The suture for my broken heart
She was solid ground for my weary feet
She was the shaman I needed all along
To find, heal, and nurture all of my broken child parts
I can rest now
Protected by her love
I can shed less tears now
Corrected by her love
And I can feel secure now
Reminded of the boundless depth of her love.

Love of My Life

I wish I knew
What I did to deserve you
Your loyalty
Your trust
Your constant attention
And dedication
To making us, US
Two pillars of strength
Two columns of light
Two beams of hope
Two dreams afloat
Two Queens in flight
I bow down to your love
My darling
I honor you for life.

CHERIL N. CLARKE

In the Quiet Hours

She finds pleasure in the pre-dawn hours of quiet solitude
In daily reflections and searches for self
She finds intimate awareness
Of her relationship with her body
Her heart
Her spirit
And whom she chooses to allow in them.
Before the bringers of anarchy marshal in
And greedy mobs cannibalize civility
She leans on the teachings of her lineage
Settles down in her temple within
To honor herself
To strengthen her resolve
To gather pieces of power only found in the quiet hours
She finds sustenance in silent breaths before sunrise
Each inhale cutting through clouds of ambiguity
Each exhale aligning into congruity
She finds joy in being still
She finds peace being instilled
She continuously discovers God and Her will
In the quiet hours.

Capacity to Love

There is a wordless song in the marrow of my bones
A song that vibrates from the matter
That is supposed to make me whole
A hymn to fill the cracks in my soul
A symphony of ethereal spirits washing over me
Cleansing me from the soot of self-doubt
From uncertainty and questioning my worth
My necessity—my value
From head to toe
Chakra to chakra
From heart, to throat, to root
And Shiva to Shakti
This song has reverberated
Ricocheted throughout my being
Zig zagging and singing
Knocking down all nagging negative perceptions of self
Until the only things left were
Purified thoughts and
Renewed strength
Universal understanding
That I am enough
As I am
And yes, my capacity to love rivals oceanic
But I can never drown or overwhelm the lover who is truly
ready to handle me.

CHERIL N. CLARKE

The Sacred Sex Worker

She stands in the gap
The brighter side of the moon
On dark nights
For lovers who have temporarily drifted apart
For singles yet to find love at all
For those dying for someone to touch them from the heart
She steps in
Steeped in compassion
Dripping with antiquity
Of the world's most basic needs
Love
And touch
And as such
She is tranquil hedonism
Free of egoism
Despite being ridiculed
Despite being misunderstood
She is motherhood
A well of nurturing
A prayer surfacing
An alchemic assertion when
She stares into heartbroken eyes and mends the pieces
She pulls souls from ditches
Willing their agony to cease
She is her own religion
She is
The sacred sex worker.

Guard's Up

No matter how good it feels
How amazing the connection
When I walk out of that door
It's over
When daydreams, vivid memories and flashbacks wash over
me
I remind myself not to feel too much
Not to get too enamored
Because at the end of the day
This is her job
And I am just a client
I am paying for these feelings
Do they even really exist?
I believe they are genuine
But even if so
I can't get caught up
Can't get entangled
Or too enamored
Because she won't catch me
If I fall for her
She's not responsible for my feelings
And doesn't care to be
She's made it clear
And that's fair.
She's got her own lover
Her own life.
I overstand.
So, in the end

CHERIL N. CLARKE

It is I who will end up shattered if I am not careful
Never fall in love with a sex worker
You'll just end up broke and broken-hearted in the end
Keep everything in that hour
Just accept that for what it is
Transactional affection
Nurturing touch from an expert
A little slice of undivided attention.

Why Is She Here?

Who are these women?
The escorts, the strippers, the tantric bodyworkers
And yes, even the mistresses
Who are they serving?
What are they fulfilling?
The lonely
The forgotten
The bored
The knotted-hearted?
Is it sex
Is it love
Is it adventure
Is it intimacy?
What are the circumstances that led to their appearance
In the lives of many
Single or married
These are the questions too rarely asked
What secret heartbreaks are these women healing?
What private pains are they mending?
What desperately needed attention are they giving?
What is the honest reason for them to be needed?
If they've entered your life
Through the back door or the front
These are the questions you can't run from
These are the ones
The ones you must confront.

CHERIL N. CLARKE

Convergence of Desire

There are six hands
Three sets of lips
Uninhibited touch
Floggers, restraints, and whips
Skin on skin like silk
Butter-soft and in sync
They buck, grind, and writhe
Blindfolded
Overwhelming the senses
Scratching and holding
Surrounded by sensations
They twist, turn, and dip
Entangle limbs
Backs bent and arched
Rocking on their secret ark.
On the rushes of fluidity
Converges a swirl of molten mother of pearl and seed
Sweat washes over ridges and veins
Moans and whimpers of multiple names
Fill the room like a fragrance
There's rhythm
There's cadence
There's pleasure in pacing
Waiting
Delaying
Euphoria and exhilaration
They live
In a moment of desires converging.

Bite the Pillow

Red lights
Candles and hot wax
Eager flesh
Silver trays of fruit and other aphrodisiacs
Bouquets of pinks flowers
A bassline and piano…a gentle drum kick
A whole mood
A whole vibe
Rhythm and hues
Bright falsetto moans
Never the blues
Brown on brown skin
From fingertips to inner thighs
And deep within
My desire is lit fuse
My breath is a pant
My moans…a purr
The taste of your skin is an orange liqueur
An intoxicating mix of god and goddess
Aphrodite and Adonis and maybe a little Ishtar
I mean, why not?
I want to give you all my love
If it's the last thing I do
I want to love you from the core of my soul
Until you feel it in your bones
I want to crawl on top and all over you
Surround you with touch until you clutch, grip, grab and
Hold the sheets
Until your groans billow into a scream

Until you feel transported to your best wet dream
Until you bite the pillow to release steam
This is a love supreme
Indulge with me.

The Lover of Your Dreams (Paradise in Hell)

If these are the last days
I will be your paradise in hell
If the streets have gone mad
I will shelter you and welcome you to my dwelling
If your head and heart are overwhelmed
I will bathe you from my well
I have an abundance of protection—enough to share
Enough to pour over you
Love-infused streams of healing intention
The opposite of fear is safety
To cease feeling afraid, you must feel secure
Step into my lair
I will cleanse you in the cure
I am holy water
My embrace is a refuge
Cascade into my arms
Say everything you've wanted say
Let it out
Let it go
Be real
Say goodbye
Say hello
Start anew
I am the altar, and your obedience to just *be* is the offering
Feel the goddess warmth
Of my almond-oiled skin
Breathe and allow yourself to sink in

To the depths of our embrace
Let your soul experience the deep pleasures
That are hidden in the art of patience
Feel the soft electricity of my touch
And awaken to the infinite possibilities of affection
Let me take my time with you
I am passion dipped in luxury
My aura is auriferous
My pillows are brocade
My robe gleams like gold
I am the queen.
I am your escape.
Get lost in me
This kind of lovemaking is outside the realm of the average
I am a journey to travel in
You are safe with me
Be free and guilt free
For letting your desires out
I am the lover of your dreams
If these are the last days
I will be your paradise in hell.

Endless Love

It's so easy to repeatedly fall in love with her
Her eyes, her smile, her dimples, her style
They ripple and radiate
Iridescence, resilience, and strength
She is the bearer of benevolence
The genesis of affection
The alpha of love
She is cosmic embodiment of female divination
Mother earth's heir to the throne
She is my air, she is my love, she is my home
When the world slows down
And her throngs of admirers fall back
Our souls reconnect
And we rediscover our power
We gallivant in the bottomless depth of our connection
Its beauties and imperfections
The scope of our humanity echoes
In the walls of our hearts
And we accept it and further commit our attention to ensure
Our love remains endless.

She's Dope

This woman is liberation
I'm drunk off the essence of her freewheeling
She might not be on a corner
But she's damn sure pleasure dealing
She has made me a fiend
She is the product and the pusher
The woman is cocaine
She is the sweetest sugar
She is sacred plant medicine
She is a trip into a nebula
This woman is kush
She is the ecstasy pulled from a bush
She is a crystal sparkling in the sun
Kissed by the goddesses
Her skin is flawless
She is a gem on top of psilocybin
She is a formidable hypothesis
She will make your forget it all
She is the object of desire
Who cannot be possessed
And only be experienced
She is The One
Indulge at your risk
In every way possible
She is certain to leave you spent.

An Avalanche of Seduction

It is time to unshackle your desires
Shine a light on your cravings
Throw gasoline on your inner fire
Let it spread on a bed of uninhibitedness
It is time for you to experience a little recklessness
I want to be your freedom
The dream you wake up to.
It's time for you to experience
Someone who thrives off her own essence
Who loves with all of her existence
Who has pledged a life-long learning commitment
To locating the hidden pathways that generate pleasure
I want to satisfy your hunger for more
Shake up your world and tear down your walls
I am well-read
I am art
I am the good news on your astrological chart
You can stop trying to learn your future
I am where you should start
I am athletic
I have stamina for days
I challenge you to take a sip
Drink from my silky bay
A night with me will haunt you for weeks
I am substance and style personified
I am an orgasmic landslide
An avalanche of seduction and I want to reveal to you
The exhilaration of becoming untangled

Becoming so undone so you can meet the real you.

Darkness Gives Birth to the Sun

I have created a space
A space for you to feel safe
Safe to admit feeling stressed out
Safe for you to allow yourself
To express vulnerability and self-doubt
A cocoon just for you and me
To melt into each other fluidly
On a rooftop at midnight reliving our childhood
We can guess the shapes of the clouds
Abandon the façade of a flawless adulthood
Where you can stop running from the spectrum of humanity
Shed your work stress
I have created an oasis into which
We can release feelings of inadequateness
A place to confess your fascinations, longings, and struggles
A realm where you don't have to muzzle the real you
I have created a space
Where you can take off your mask
Walk away from the hustle
Sway with me in my atmosphere
I want to talk all night
Until the darkness gives birth to the sun
Let's hold hands until first light.

CHERIL N. CLARKE

In a Stranger's Arms

I felt loved and nurtured
Despite my nerves, I felt seen and I felt heard
In a stranger's arms
I fell in love with the danger
Of rediscovering myself
The beauty, the broken, and the gritty little pieces
Some of which
I hadn't seen in years.
In a stranger's arms
I became enamored with myself
At the possibilities of how it would have felt
To have been living out loud all along
To have embraced my light and my dark full-on
To have explored my kinks and my virtues
To have sung my soul's songs.
In a stranger's arms
I relaxed in a galaxy of a moment
Became vulnerable enough to crack open
The universe of my being
It was a scary yet liberating feeling
I cried like a shy child on her mother's breasts
Tears of joy and some of sorrow.
Many of relief from dropping the weight.
In a stranger's arms
I was electrified at the possibilities of me
Of the possibilities of tomorrow
If I hold the confidence to just be.

Withdrawal

I still savor the taste of you
The flavor of your cocoa-colored skin
I miss the scent of you
Your aroma of desire
The wild look of fire in your walnut eyes
I miss the way you used to seep into my waters
The way your steel was strong enough to remain ablaze
In my fleshy reservoir
The way we'd combust and comeback
Like loving immortals
I miss my all-nighters with you
The morning afters
The lazy, tender afternoons
Our hedonistic paradise for two
Tell me you hear me
Tell me you feel me
Tell me that you see me
Calling out for you…

CHERIL N. CLARKE

The Exhibitionist

She wanted to do it outside
Ever the exhibitionist
She wanted to relish in a euphoria
Of being spied upon by foreign eyes
Of performing
Winding
And grinding
Of licking
And sucking
And bucking
Of gripping and holding
Onto one another.
She wanted to float
On a flood tide under a full moon
Below shadowy covers of night
Beneath sparkles of cosmic luminosity
She wanted to indulge her hunger
Satisfy her sexual curiosity
To abate and advance
Between the vulnerability of darkness and domination
And an erotic nirvana
Shared with many partners
To consecrate her beautifully fluid space
Converge the yearnings of her body
Her spirit
And her mind
She wanted to do it outside
Far away from hiding

BITE THE PILLOW

To be herself
Unveiled and unleashed
Letting her existence put on a show
An inspiration piece
Of how deliciously beautiful sacred sexuality could be.

A Taste of Paradise

She tastes like passion fruit infused rum
Hazelnut skin
Walnut eyes
Pink lips and ivory smile
She is surreal
In this world but not of it
She is from a clandestine tribe of women
Born at the altar of love
Steeped in skills of erotic wonder
She is a gift to the world
With garlands of flowers adorning her hair
She basks at the center her own universe
Surrounded by drummers
Singers
Decorated dancers—throngs of admirers chanting
Panting, grasping, hoping
For a touch or taste of her existence
Goddess vibes
She is emotional richness
Spiritual abundance
Physical thunder
An oasis of supple pleasure
She is a roving treasure
Catch her if you can.

Authentic and Uncivilized

She called it a fragrance
Not a smell
There's a difference and I felt it when she said it
She said it was slippery
That it glistened
That she was smitten
And that I'm addicting.
She said that one touch
One graze
One contact
One taste
Would immediately lead her into orgasm.
The words stopped me cold
Truth be told
That's when I realized
That words of affection just might be my love language
I've never needed to hear 'I love you,'
But the vocalization of a lover's desires
Set my soul on fire
It's one area where I don't want it neat or proper
I don't want it predictable
I want it authentic
Uncivilized
Unequivocal
Tell me how you want it
How you like it
When you need it
Never hide it

I want to hear and feel it vibrating
I want your inner thoughts to strike like thunder and
lightning
Please, *please*, don't hide them.

Her Lips Taste Like Poetry

I feel her in my chest
This woman is so much
Her existence is a benediction
She has unknowingly helped me break so many addictions
To limiting beliefs
To restrictive ways of being
To standing still in potential
Instead of stepping into actualization.
She brought a torch and lit up the dark corners of my heart
She is the Spirit
She is the One
The one who brought me back to life
From the edge of apathy
She is the one who encouraged an eruption of disruption
To fall in love with myself again
With the world too
She's the gospel
Her lips taste like poetry
Her voice is a hymnal
Her fragrance makes me hungry
For a taste of the ultimate freedom
She has made a home in my rib cage
She may have been there all along
She is an eternal whisper
Waiting quietly in the wings of life
For me to stop and listen.

CHERIL N. CLARKE

A Feast of Femininity

Trench coat and fishnet stockings
That's how I'll show up at your front door
And your hotel suite
The slice of seduction you need
To appease your sweet tooth
I am a feast of femininity
Quelling your craving for sexual healing
Draped in bespoke lingerie
Exquisitely tailored
Fitting like a second skin
I am a temple for you to sit and worship in
A force with which to be reckoned - I am
The answer to your kinky prayers
The object of your secret stares
Now here for your adoration
Here for your feet kisses
Here for your fetishes
Here to fulfill your dark desires
I am here for your bended knee glances
Up to the goddess.

The Challenge of Your Love

Falling for you
Was like descending 10,000 feet per second
Heart beating and thrashing
Winds of self-reflection whiplashing
Adrenaline rushing
Eyes bulging
Unable to unsee
What the challenge of your love has done within me
I felt my mind crashing yet clinging
To "refined" versions of myself
To sterility
And respectability
I struggled to let go
Despite tasting the juicy sweetness
Of authentically living's possibilities
I was afraid
Because conformity
Seemed to be all I'd known
But your quiet gaze
And resolute gale of being
Disintegrated my superficial existence
Blew to bits
I've been reborn in raw honesty
It hurt
Before it the beauty of it all
Began to reveal itself and flirt
And dance, and seduce me.
Falling for you was looking into a mirror I didn't want to see

Hearing echoes of youthful voices
Of desires and dreams
Snuffed out by others' influence and regency.
Falling for you was like tumbling into a soul-port of
opportunities for pleasure
If I could just go
If I could just be free
If I could just be wild
If I could just be me
The challenge of your love has freed me
Because I gave in to the fall.

The Smoke

She knows she's the smoke
At the tip of the stick
A signal
A beacon
A swirling alert to the gods and goddesses
That I'm ready but afraid
Still, the time is now
This is it.
Time to own my divinity
Honor my sacred
Release my burdens and my guilt...
All shame of being
Time to release them
And let my emotional scars
Be reimagined as wisdom stripes
As body art
She is the energy behind my introspection
The light that guides me to my ancestral connection
Reminding me of the strength and depth of my roots
Illuminating the potential of my power
Reminding me that I am the flower and the fruit
She is the smoke.

CHERIL N. CLARKE

Run Away with Me

Into the fields
Up and down the rolling hills
Where the crickets chirp and birds pip
Where acres of wildflowers bloom
And honeybees buzz
Where hundred-year-old trees dance and plume
And browned leaves carpet the earth's floor.
Run away with me
Into the scent of sandalwood and peach trees
To the chorus and melodies of rushing creeks
Let's get wet...
Run away with me
To a place where fresh-water flows from the mountaintops
And lush leaves tower from the tips of bamboo stalks
Where forestry fragrances the air
And wild mushrooms pop through the soil
Where bachelor fireflies glow and toil
Run away with me, my love
To sun kisses from God
In wide swaths of succulent land
Where hummingbirds perch on bergamot
And granite rock glistens around the tranquil ponds
Run away with me to freedom
To beauty and bounty
Harvest me in the wild
Chase me as I run naked and carefree
Barefoot, with orchid petals at my feet
Please, run away with me.

Like Open Water

Wade into me like open water
Like endless warmth
And boundless possibilities
Like infinite comfort.
Explore my curves like a riverbend
The peaks and valleys of coconut-oiled skin
Inhale my scent and raise the temperature
Until sweat dips and slopes
Until it drips down collarbones
Runs over shoulders
Gathers in little puddles
Into the folds and creases of muscle
Of my strength as a woman
Until it collapses into the pillows beneath us
Surrender to the moment and know that
Our alchemy as a coupling
Is all that matters
Be still and let the warmth of my breath
Ripple over you like a tropical breeze
Slow love…you can drop all of your masks with me
Abandon your disguises
Let your self-consciousness *wash away*
Get rid of anxiety about your desires
About your kinks, your lusts, your yearnings, and your
curiosities
Let them all go
Like glaciers melting into an amorous stream
I am the nurturing elements of open water

I just want you to float with me...

Apologies

I'm sorry
For being so much
That it scared you away
For coming off as entitled
To your time
Your affection
To your vibe
But at least you could have said goodbye.

CHERIL N. CLARKE

The Rebellious Woman

Head wrapped in a red turban
Arms tattooed
Lips pierced
She is decorated in freedom
She is a cultural homebrew
Warrior woman in the spirit of Oya
She strikes like lightening
Unafraid to live or die
Fearless and ready to bear arms
She is an existential riot
Running through life in the nude – she is a lit fuse
The antithesis of the masses – those shrouded by conformity
Her assuredness makes people uncomfortable
Because she is so damned incomparable
She can never go unnoticed
This woman is brazen
Loud, untamed, and confident in her existence
She is a REBEL
A wonderland of courage and freedom
And a nightmare to authorities
A whole 360, creating strength out of her vulnerabilities
She is an electrifying tonic
Boundless and free-flowing
A luscious river of liberation
The master torch to light up the world in search of freedom
This woman is everything
She is the embodiment of rebellion
And I'm addicted.

A Delicious Tease

She was worth the trouble
Worth the growing pains
Worth the risk and the fight
To abandon all of my yesterdays
To leave it all behind
To create a new way of living
A soul-satisfying way of being
She was the most paradoxical gift
Her gaze seemed innocent enough at first
Like sea foam rolling on to dry land
She was a delicious tease
A deep-sea of roiling possibilities beckoning me
Daring me to expand my consciousness
Magnify my awareness
To love with complete abandon
More adventurously than I'd ever done
She was enchantingly disobedient
The creator of her own world
A towering tribute to the power of beauty
The embodiment of freedom
A monument of organic sensuality
Sticky sweet
Breaking all of the rules
She lives in the fibers of my spirit
I cannot contain myself when imagining her
Unforgettable and ever-complicit
Always on the quest to live in orgasmic bliss.

CHERIL N. CLARKE

Pleasure Unbound

Smudged makeup and disheveled hair
Crooked eyelashes
Shouldn't have even worn them here
Twisted bedsheets and pillows everywhere
The morning after...
Scratches on my back and sides
A little bruising on my hamstrings and thighs
It was a merry-go-round of slow entrancement
Spun into fast, bed-rattling
Passive-aggressive
Lively and lazy
A tug of war of lovemaking
All night
Building up to an unearthly dismantling
Of all concepts of time
We swirled in the forever of now
In pleasure unbound
Now here we are at the dawn of a new day
My legs wrapped around you like vines clinging to a tree
Your body is my fiefdom
Wherever we lay is my queendom
And I want to love you like the ocean
Constant, engrossing, and strong
Calm on the surface
Dark and tense below
Washing over you and pulling you under
Pulling you under
Pulling you under...

A Renaissance of Pleasure

Restless
Full of stamina
She is the most adulterous fantasy
Just as much as she is a classical dream
Slim thick with hella intellect
She likes her women dominant
And her men submissive
Impatient for love
She is tired of waiting
Tired of wanting
Done with watching others get what they want
Just take her already
She's been ready
Make it a renaissance of pleasure
A comeback for passion
Throw gasoline on the embers
Reignite your hunger for one another
Paint a new picture to fill in what's faded over time
She's restless and full of stamina
Wanting you to mark her as your territory
To love her until she's out of breath
To drain and pour into her fountain
To penetrate her to the deepest depth
She's waiting for you
Don't let her slip away.

Run

You always run away
When your presence matters the most
When conversations go below the surface
And unfiltered emotions are revealed.
You always bow out
Before the round is over
Before your back can touch a corner
As though finishing a conversation
Is an absolute horror.
You always flee
When I want desperately
For you to stay and talk to me
To show me you care
To display even the slightest interest
In my depth
To ask me "why" about anything
But it seems as though all you want is surface love
A little flirting and casual fun
Maybe it's me who should run.

Cocoon in Love

His words are like an embrace
Carving out a safe space
For me to curl up and cocoon in love.

CHERIL N. CLARKE

The Butterfly Kiss

You have needled your way
Into the consciousness of my veins
Only to flex and fly away
To course through me like adrenaline
You were an unexpected butterfly
Purple with yellow edges
A disease and a medicine
A pin prick that made my heart bleed
I hate feeling needy
I despise feeling stupid
I loathe the addiction
And the delusion
Of thinking I mean something to you
"Us" is just an illusion.

Black Bird in a White Sky

It took countless days
Of trying and failing
Before she built enough resolve
To stop feeding one-sided friendships
And love affairs
To fly away from uncomfortable
Yet familiar nests
And soar like a black bird in a white sky
Wind in her face
Moving through resistance and the uncertainty of it all
Through inner turmoil and limiting beliefs
Feelings of unworthiness
That kept her treading in a cycle of
Excitement, disappointment, hurt and frustration, and back
to excitement again...
She's flying away from emotional *scraps*
And the after-thought hellos
That others dole
Away from self-absorbed individuals
The journey is long
But she finds strength in accepting that people come and go
That she doesn't own them
Or have authority of how they spend their time
The journey is long indeed
She's learned how to acknowledge her negative feelings but
not live in them
Learned how to love letting *go*
Just as much as the intoxicating experiences of discovery.

CHERIL N. CLARKE

When It's Over

It was over so fast I didn't have time to cry
Didn't have time to process
Didn't have a moment to ask why
Some lovers come into your life hard and fast
Their time is brief
But their impression is eternal
And though your heart aches, and you yearn for them in
earnest
You have to let go
You have to move on
You have to accept it for what it was
And be grateful it happened at all.

LOST

I close my eyes and get LOST in memories
Of rolling with her
In Ecstasy
In Bliss
In Nirvana
Swimming in reveries
Of how she enlivened my spirit
Electrified my soul
Of what she did for me
I would walk 10,000 miles for her
For just one more trip
One more journey into heaven
One more chance
To feel her fingertips against my skin
I'll never forget her as long as I live
She is a paradise
The breath of life
A beam of light
A flag of freedom flying high
The joy in the awareness of now
A concentration of pleasure
A peak that can't be measured
A concatenation of satisfaction
Whew
I close my eyes and get LOST in the memories...

Worthy

There should always come a moment
When you stop being in love with a fantasy
And cherish your reality
When you stop being grateful
For scraps of affection
From inattentive lovers
For whom you are an afterthought--a blip in their attention
There should come a day
When you see your self-worth
And feel your inner strength
When you realize your value
And taste the sweetness of freedom
From abandoning the projections of perfection
You naively put on others
Who were always unworthy
There should come a time
When you stop lowering your standards
Stop remaining where you are unseen
For the true glory that you are
Take control of your heart
Take control of your life
Demand better
Because you are worthy.

Switch

Sometimes I carry the whip
Sometimes I'm wearing the collar
While I love the feeling of being in control
There's also splendor in surrender
Of falling into the enthralling
Middle
Of everything.
Passion
Play
Trust and vulnerability
Domination and power
Unpredictability is delectable in a world of boring conformity
Switch…

CHERIL N. CLARKE

Aftercare

I want to drink you like Holy Water
Taste your sweat
Taste your skin
Take you farther than you've ever thought possible
Farther than you've ever been
I want to reel you into my energy field
Take your breath away
Make your skin tingle
Pull you into my aura
Into my tailor-made atmosphere for pleasure
Into my hedonistic suite of whips, chains, crosses, cages and
leather
I want to sink my nails into your skin
Scrape and scratch a little
Mark you up so others know that you're mine
Grab fists full of your hair
And choke you just a little…
Command you to your knees
Order you to worship me
To embrace the impact of paddles
Until you reach subspace
Until you're ecstatic
Then we lounge in languid affection
Breathing in sync
Holding onto each other tightly
While I caress your body
Wipe you down with warm towels
And express my gratitude for your trust.

A Hedonistic Heaven

If I could make love to you
I would make it a multi-day event
Invoke your fantasies and ease your apprehensions
Stimulate your mind and create a bespoke dimension
I would explore your body like a galaxy of beauty
Guide you into a space between light and dark
Suspend us in ecstasy
Admire you like cosmic art
I would feed your carnal desires
Satisfy the hungers of your soul
Ignite your wildest thoughts
Encourage you to indulge
If I could make love to you
I would slow things all the way down
I would make time stop
Get rid of all distractions
Lead you into an orgasmic state of rapture
Into a perpetual state of pleasure
From night until morning
Afternoon into the evening
From dusk until dawn
I would nurture you with attention
Tend to you until your body tingled and rocked
I would bring you to the edge of a hedonistic heaven
Hold open the door when god knocks
Introduce you to another world
Where insecurities and shame do not exist
Where you can feel at home in your body

CHERIL N. CLARKE

Where your skin melts into mine
And we wade into a river of ecstasy
The pleasure waters that lie in the folds of my skin
If only I could make love to you…

At the Altar of Love

Dim lights
Votive candles in red holders
Coco mango incense
Rose petals and lavender buds
Swirling smoke curling above
An altar of love
Subtle drums beat through fragrant air
I trance out...
Rock and sway
Eyes closed
Breathing steady and full
Deep
Feeling the electrifying tingle
Of my skin becoming more and more alive
With each breath
With each involuntary, yet divinely guided movement
I sink deeper
Into the calm waters of my mind
Enveloped in reflection and guidance
And inner peace
This is bliss.

CHERIL N. CLARKE

Oceans of Seduction

She is a strange phenomenon
Mysterious and majestic
Enchanting and infuriating
She teases with her smile
Intoxicates with her laugh
And overpowers with her intellect
She brings me to my knees
Sets me on fire
Knowing she is the water
She douses me
Feeding my desire
But stops short of quenching my thirst
She is a licentious libation
She keeps me wanting
Falling
Sinking
Deeper
Into her oceans of seduction.

A Rare Goddess on Earth

Slow kissing her was like nursing on consciousness
Every tongue connection
Every jaw caress
Every moan
Every skin tingle and inner thigh tremble
Lifted me higher
Pulled me deeper
I wanted to lay in her arms forever
Enlightened by her presence
Comforted by her nurturing
Captivated by her energy
Invigorated just by watching her way of living
She had a zest for existing
That couldn't be extinguished
A peace
A comfort
A way of being that was pure sweetness
Like sugar cane under an island tree
She was an escape
A taste of freedom
A kiss from the sun
A cool summer breeze
This woman was *beautiful*
From the projection of her aura
Down to the embers of her soul
Wifey material
A rare Goddess on earth
She was more precious than gold.

Her Name is Love

Just one glance
One gaze
One utterance from her honeysuckle lips of my name
Draws me into a new atmosphere
Into the horizon
Above the clouds
Into bliss, and I am high...I am High...I am **HIGH**
Floating on an intoxicating vibration of passion
Levitating above water
On air
In the *wind*...
Just one graze of strands of her hair
One taste of her strawberry nectar skin
And I am drawn in
My attraction to her is involuntary
Primal and instinctual...
Dangerous
I could fight it with all my might and still lose
Her presence is blinding yet illuminating
A lamp after years in the dark
The divine feminine
The unfiltered truth
The unfettered root of life
Her name is Love.

Energy

I can feel you through my fingertips
When I caress my leg
Rub my feet
Graze my sides
I can feel the currents of your energy imprint flowing through
me
Your intentions
Your will
They're still here
Whatever love you gifted to me is persistent
Barreling through my resistance
Optimistic
It's surprising
Our harmonizing
Our vibes and
Distance be damned
I'm thriving
I've never experienced anything like this.

CHERIL N. CLARKE

Interstellar

Outstretched and vulnerable
I collapse under the weight of her body
Pressed into mine
A beautiful heaviness covers me
And I become more comfortable
Wrapped in a cocoon of safety
Until I go limp
Letting go
I begin melting
Submerging into the sacred layers of myself
Down to the original atom
I am a single cell
And she is the big bang.

Rhythm and Blues

Infatuation wraps me in rhythm and blues
Like a silky solo over a sultry bass line
Accented by taps on a snare – a ticking reminder
My heart beats
It thunders
And booms
Thinking of us.
Of her.
Of me.
Of him.
New feelings blossom and bloom
Remembering how we consume one another without
costume
Without fear
Without guilt
Without concern
Without excessive thinking and analyzing
We flow
Our progression shifts into a symphony
Too soon interrupted by reality
And I go from the highest high
To the lowest low
Infatuation wraps me in rhythm and blues.

Gratitude

She stops the world and defies gravity
With intention and touch
Compassion and connection
She lifts a thousand pounds of pressure off me
Allowing me to float on a blanket of black air
Weightless
Gliding in the ether
Aimless
To drift toward Orion and a gibbous moon
I feel myself splitting at the surface
Tearing along the seams
In a state of inexplicable consciousness
Preparing for expansion
Getting ready a full bloom
I am rolling
Uninhibited
I am in ecstasy
Fully stimulated
I am wholly indebted to her generosity of love
Of attentiveness
Of diligence
And of her courage to own, indulge, and share that at which
is she is so gifted.

Gratitude II

I adore your mind
The way it bends and curves
Its flow down in the depths
And risings beyond the sky
I love the seat of your soul
Your devotion to exploring emotion
Of yours
And mine – through pleasure and insanity – invigorates me
I am enamored with your commitment to honoring the
breadth of humanity
Your essence holds me…folds me into a cradle of safety
And I'm filled with gratitude
Thank you.

CHERIL N. CLARKE

She is a Dream

She is the answer to the prayers I am too afraid to vocalize
The type of woman with whom I dream of spending an
evening
Barefoot and barely clothed on a rooftop
Under the moon
Covered by stars
On summer's night
Enjoying a comfortable breeze
With no humidity
Only humility and conversation
Exploration of the stuff that is us
That is life
About philosophy and freedom and love and trust
She is a dream
A figment of my imagination
She is a fantasy
As this experience can never be.

Open Up

It's the spontaneity I long for
The element of surprise
A little risk
Less control
More abandon into the abyss
Of exhilaration
Into a space of unfurling and unraveling
Becoming unfastened
To fly freely with passion
On trapezes of great suspension
Above it all
Swing. Split. Spin. Dip.
To open up for life.

Power

I am so distracted by your power
Your voice
Your stance
Your vulnerability
Your glance
You are a mountain at which I stand to marvel
The spark and sparkle of the universe
In a single human body
You are strength
The Talented Tenth
Simply exceptional
I am hypnotized by the centuries of wisdom behind your eyes
The playful youth of your smile
I want to feel all of your glory
I want to see you come from behind the podium
Step into the scarlet garden of followers
Admirers who await to adore you
For uplifting and enlightening them
For revealing the potential of their lives to them
Oh, my Goddess, I am so rapt by your power.

Dangerous Water

I've found myself planking at the mouth of her river
My lips
So eager to taste and sip her nectar
They quiver
But I hold back
I restrain my desire
I waver at the gates of pleasure
Because I know if I dive in
I won't be able to quit her
She is a universe unto herself
Made of pure love
The vibration of her voice
A hedonistic serenade
Calling me
Haunting me
I debate risking it all for her
But I don't
My better judgment – a sentry sent to protect me prevents me
From drowning in her dangerous water.

CHERIL N. CLARKE

Magical Water

His fingertips explore me like curious strangers
Eager to conquer a foreign land
But slowly
Until I give the command
The okay
The permission
To travel the divinity of my skin
Six dozen candles set the room aglow
Yellow and red rose petals adorn the pillows
The sheets
The floor
To him, I am healing
I am health
I am balance
A refuge.
A phallus riser.
The River Niger
A basin of magical water
He has waited a lifetime to devour.

Oceans

There are so many little actions you've taken
That intoxicate me
So many thoughtful moments
That mean mountains to me
Enriched my spirit
Caressed my heart
Quieted my raging soul
The tears I cry are of affection and relief
But they also contain traces of fear and mourning
Yet in a new day
The old me wakes up in the morning
To an evolved me
The journey
A mix of joy, appreciation, and excitement
There are oceans in my teardrops
What a release.

CHERIL N. CLARKE

Out of This World

She takes my breath away
Inhales and exhales
In a way that has us swept away
Into a surreal atmosphere
Of unbridled joy
Unrivaled euphoria
Our love is steadfast and enduring
Eternal and beyond the comprehension of the average
It is a staggering gathering of gratitude
Of devotion
A supernatural love potion
We've lived through every experience
Catapulted through space and time
High-jumped over the trivial
Torn down worldly confines
Broken rules and restrictions
That are meaningless unless defined by us
She is the song of my heart
Her gaze is a kiss to my soul
Her loyalty is legendary
This love is a rapture—it never gets old
She is my best friend
Just the sound of her name sends a vibration
That calls for an ascent
She is out of this world

Celestial Lovers

I'm attracted to her through primal instinct
Him too
Like still water between mountains
I relish in being flanked by a god and a goddess
It is grounding.
Let the earth be our bed
Let natural hedonism loom overhead
Like a cosmic cover
Let's float in the rainbows of the cosmos
As celestial lovers.

CHERIL N. CLARKE

In an Unguarded Moment

I stumbled into pleasure
In an unguarded moment
I fell into joy
With closed eyes and breaths so deep
My chest expanded in a slow creep
Upward, and around and down
To surround me with the surreal.
In an unguarded moment
She penetrated my being from afar
Pushing aside the shutters that I'd placed around my heart
She opened my eyes to the splendor of consciousness
To the exhilaration in surrender
To the promise of ascending into love
Into heaven
Into the sublime
In an unguarded moment
I found trust and awareness
I found ecstasy and meaning
I learned to let go of some goals
So that I could relish the individual moments—the steps
As each one is its own gift.

A Divine Fire

There is a part of her that is lovingly burned into my soul
Imprinted in my heart
Solidified in my spirit
She found my abandoned embers
And nurtured them into a flame
That blossomed into a wildfire
And blazes to this day
I am a divine fire.

She kissed my tears and pulled me close
I felt her heartbeat against my temple
As I lay my head against her chest
And rested
In the arms of love
The hands of rejuvenation
The release of pain
Was replaced with a spiritual branding of love
I've now spread at home and to the world.

CHERIL N. CLARKE

Shock the System

Be different
Be enrapturing
Be enthralling
In a world full of boredom, banality and carbon copy
personalities
Be radical
Shatter generalities
Embrace whimsicality
Or don't
And I will.

Goddess Rising (From Within)

Like a mountain rising from the bottom of the sea
She is on her way
To reclaim her children
To uplift her sisters
To nurture her lovers
She is arriving.
After a millennium of rest
She is arising from a mystical slumber
Vibrating and pulsating
Radiating light over arid wastelands
Pillaged and disrespected
By greed and the tangled mess of colonization.
She is on her way and
The return of her gaze
Will shine light on the shadows.
The comeback of her influence
Will cradle and heal the wounded
The homecoming of her intellect
Will remind modern women
That they were warriors all along
That they were queens all along
She is a vital energy
A natal home—the very arms of *love*
With morning glories gathered at her feet
A jeweled crown at her peak
She is a paradise of possibilities too long buried within
Her presence is ammunition for change and elevation

She is returning to extinguish your anguish and reignite your dreams.

Weekend Love

If I could make love to you
I would make it a multi-day event
I have exhausted my imagination
Coming up with ways to get to know you
To see you
To feel you
To sense and indulge
In the sweet butter-almond that is your skin
I want to stimulate every inch
From the delicate hair on your forearms
To the layers beneath your pores
I want to caress your soul
Pour my love into you
With attentiveness
With touch
With kisses
With amorous gazes
Nose to skin inhaling
I want to take my time with you
Lift you out of your body until you float
Into the ether
Just below the constellation

CHERIL N. CLARKE

Intensity

I am so at home in myself
Revitalized
Invigorated
And hungry.
I want to invite you in
Gently guide you through sensory deprivation
Take you deep
Below the layer of mundane chatter and basic orgasms
Deep
Into the ecstasy of consciousness
Into the darkness
Where you'll find the fire of your soul
Into the stillness
Where you'll sense the subtle vibrations of euphoria
Into seclusion
Where you'll discover the joys entrancing love
I want to bring forth a tsunami of satisfaction
A throbbing pulse of rhythmic patterns
Unleash bites and scratches
Grab fistfuls hair
And coax deep, open-mouth breaths
You are so many layers of beautiful
I want to explore all of your textures and creases
Your ridges and folds
All of the surfaces and some of the openings of your body
I want to cultivate a massive build up energy
Make your entire body an erogenous zone
Journey the past your skin down to your nerves

BITE THE PILLOW

Make you feel me down in the marrow of your bones
Intensity
I live for it.

END

If you enjoyed the book, please consider leaving a review on Amazon.com.

Please also consider posting a photo of you holding the book to your favorite social media account and tagging any of the following:

@CherilNClarke on Facebook
@cheril.n.clarke on Instagram
@cherilnc on Twitter
@cherilnicole on TikTok

For more work by Cheril please visit cherilnclarke.com. There you will find poetry, short stories, novels, stage plays, music, and more. THANK YOU for your support. It means the world to me!